RED HOT
GOURMET

COLE GROUP

Both U.S. and metric units are provided for all recipes in this book. Ingredients are listed with U.S. units on the left and metric units on the right. The metric quantities have been rounded for ease of use; as a result, in some recipes there may be a slight difference (approximately ½ ounce or 15 grams) between the portion sizes for the two types of measurements.

© 1995 Cole Group

Cover Photograph: Michael Lamotte

Cole Group
1330 N. Dutton Ave., Ste. 103
Santa Rosa, CA 95401
(800) 959-2717 (707) 526-2682
FAX (707) 526-2687

Printed in Hong Kong

G F E D C B A
1 0 9 8 7 6 5

ISBN 1-56426-800-4
Library of Congress Catalog Card Number 94-40118

Distributed to the book trade by Publishers Group West

Cole books are available for quantity purchases for sales promotions, premiums, fund-raising, or educational use. For more information on *Red Hot Gourmet* or other Cole's Cooking Companion books, please write or call the publisher.

CONTENTS

RED HOT AND GETTING HOTTER

*H*ot news flash! Salsa's edging out catsup as
the universal condiment of choice; competition
at international chili cook-offs is rivaling that
of major sports events; searching for new
varieties of hot chiles has become a culinary
obsession; and heat-loving aficionados every-
where are relishing the global warming
wrought by the hottest food trend on the
planet. Fire-powered fare is here to stay.

A PASSION FOR FIRE-POWERED FARE

The passionate pursuit of foods that make us gasp for breath and perspire is nothing new. Early attempts at food preservation often involved liberal applications of pepper and other strong-tasting seasonings—the same ingredients used to help mask the taste of decay when victuals had passed their prime. Many of the hottest cuisines originated in very warm climates, where particular foods have long been revered for their ability to induce sweating, thereby triggering a kind of natural air-conditioning when the sweat evaporates. Throughout history pepper, garlic, chiles, and other hot foods have been acclaimed as digestives, antiseptics, antidepressants, and even aphrodisiacs.

Practical benefits aside, certain edibles possess an irresistible quality that keeps human palates begging for more. The fascination with hot stuff—foods capable of producing a mix of pleasure and pain—has developed into a hot love affair, and it's getting hotter every day.

SOURCES OF HEAT

Cuisines the world over rely on certain ingredients with a reputation for feistiness to add heat, not to mention exciting flavor. Just as the names of these foods vary from culture to culture, so do individual tolerances for heat and spiciness: What's exquisitely hot to you may not seem hot at all to someone else. In preparing the recipes in this book, let your own taste and tolerance level be your guide. Adapt the recipes to suit yourself, adding more or less of the following heat sources:

ONIONS AND GARLIC

Eaten raw, both onions and garlic release a strong-tasting acid. Cooked at low heat, the acid breaks down and the harshness dissipates. Most varieties of onions and garlic have powerful personalities but are easy to get along with when handled properly. Fresh, firm onions and young, ivory-colored heads of garlic provide the best flavor.

Mustard

The seeds of the mustard plant are virtually flavorless and odorless. But when crushed and steeped 15 minutes in water or other liquid, mustard can be blistering in its effects—literally. The volatile oils in mustard were traditionally considered powerful medicine for a number of ailments, with mustard poultices and foot baths among the most common remedies.

Prepared mustards made from yellow, brown, or black mustard seed run the gamut from mild table varieties to fiery Asian blends. Wasabi, a fire-breathing cousin to mustard, is often served with sushi and other Japanese dishes.

Horseradish

A harmless-looking, brown-skinned root with white flesh, this member of the cabbage family packs a ferocious punch. Bottled horseradish is somewhat milder than the freshly grated root, which can send a heat wave raging through the nose and sinuses. *Note:* The amounts of horseradish given in recipes in this book are for the bottled variety, unless stated otherwise. If you substitute freshly grated horseradish, start with less than half the amount given and add more if you wish.

Ginger

Ginger imparts a refreshingly clean, hot taste that adds sparkle to sweet and spicy foods alike. It is available fresh, pickled, candied, and powdered. *Note:* For the recipes in this book, powdered ginger is not an acceptable substitute for fresh ginger.

Pepper

A member of the *Piper nigrum* family, pepper is available in three forms: black peppercorns (the result of drying ripe pepper berries); white (produced by hulling the ripe berries); and green peppercorns (made by pickling the immature berries). Pepper's hot bite and flavor can't be duplicated; like mustard, it releases its heat and flavor only when cracked or ground.

CHILE

Chiles are the hot-blooded relatives of sweet, mild bell peppers, both members of the genus *Capsicum*. Hot chiles, fresh or dried, are among the most potent of all heat sources.

The amount of heat in chiles varies (depending upon the variety, growing conditions, and method of processing). Chiles have 60 percent of the substance that makes them hot—capsaicin—in the ribs and veins, 30 percent in the seeds, and 10 percent in the skin. Because small chiles have a proportionately larger volume of ribs and seeds (the hottest areas) than larger chiles, they usually pack more firepower. One of the hottest is the tiny tabasco, the main ingredient in the famous bottled condiment from Louisiana. Chiles also vary in size (from short to long), shape (from blocky to slim), and color (from pale green to yellow, orange, or red.)

Some of the most commonly available fresh chiles in U.S. markets are shown on the opposite page. Beginning at the top left and proceeding clockwise are *New Mexico* (hot), *poblano* (mild), *red jalapeño* (hot), *serrano* (very hot), and *guero* (hot). A number of these and other chiles are common to a variety of cuisines all over the world, although they may be referred to by other names.

In addition to the multitude of different names for the same chiles, the similiarity of varieties can be confusing. For example, the habanero, an H-bomb of a chile native to the Yucatán peninsula, differs slightly in color and flavor from the equally potent Jamaican Scotch Bonnet. Both chiles have their zealous fans, but the two are generally regarded as different varieties of the same species and can be substituted for one another. *Note:* A chile by any other name is just as hot; always exercise caution in handling and tasting any chile, especially if it is unfamiliar.

RECIPES AND TECHNIQUES FOR THE RED HOT GOURMET

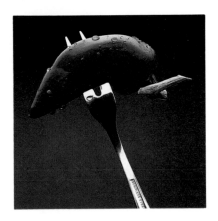

*A*ny cook can become a red hot gourmet. It's a matter of selecting authentic ingredients, mastering basic techniques, and applying them to well-crafted recipes like the ones developed for this book and the adaptations you'll create yourself. From Szechuan dipping sauce to Thai hot and sour soup, roast beef with horseradish, or Texas-style chili, you'll find more than 50 red hot recipes to tingle your mouth, clear your head, and warm your soul.

SPICY SEASONERS: SAUCES AND CONDIMENTS

Szechuan sauce for dipping, smoky barbecue sauce for brushing over ribs, Indonesian sambal for stirring into soups and rice dishes, Thai curry paste for making stews and stir-frys, chile pickles, and cayenne-spiked pecans—these powerful little potions and fiery nibbles wake up the senses and let you know you're alive. Use the following collection of sauces and condiments to add zip to whatever's on the menu.

Sambal Bajak

This popular Indonesian fried red-chile sauce is typically added to rice or stirred into soups. Warning: This sauce is potent, so use it sparingly.

8	macadamia nuts	8
¼ lb	fresh red chiles	115 g
1	onion, peeled and quartered	1
4 cloves	garlic, peeled	4 cloves
½ tsp	shrimp paste (see page 55)	½ tsp
1 tbl	brown sugar	1 tbl
2 tbl	oil	2 tbl
1	salam leaf or curry leaf, optional (see page 55)	1
¼ cup	water	60 ml

1. To prepare in a mortar, pound nuts to a coarse paste. Mince chiles, onion, and garlic and add to mortar with shrimp paste and sugar. Pound mixture to a coarse paste. To prepare in a food processor, combine macadamia nuts, chiles, onion, garlic, shrimp paste, and sugar, and process to a coarse paste. Add 1 or 2 tablespoons of water if necessary to facilitate blending.

2. In a small skillet or saucepan, heat oil over medium heat. Add chile paste and salam or curry leaf and cook, stirring, until fragrant. Add the water and continue cooking until water has evaporated and oil begins to separate. Serve warm or at room temperature, or store in a covered jar in the refrigerator.

Makes 1 cup (250 ml).

SAMBAL ULEK

When fresh hard-to-find red chiles are available, it pays to buy extra and preserve them as a paste. This fresh red-chile paste is traditionally made in a mortar, but a food processor or blender is a real timesaver.

¼ lb	fresh red chiles	115 g
1 tsp	salt	1 tsp
1 tsp	mild vinegar (optional)	1 tsp

1. To prepare in a mortar, pound chiles and salt to a coarse paste. To prepare in a blender or food processor, chop chiles to a coarse paste; add salt partway through blending.

2. Transfer to a jar and store covered in a cool place. It will keep for up to 2 weeks; for longer storage, add vinegar to cover and refrigerate.

Makes approximately ½ cup (125 ml).

SOUTHEAST ASIAN SAMBALS

The word sambal in Indonesia and Malaysia can refer to a dish cooked with chile or to a wide range of chile-based condiments, including sambal ulek (see recipe above). Used in seasoning pastes and sauces, sambal ulek also is a handy substitute for fresh chiles. A Dutch firm produces a bottled version (the label carries the old spelling—oelek) that is widely available. Sambal Bajak (see recipe on page 13) adds nuts, onions, and garlic to the basic chile paste, which is then fried to intensify the flavors.

SZECHUAN DIPPING SAUCE

This versatile dipping sauce works well with all types of Asian foods. For an easy appetizer, serve with romaine spears for scooping up the sauce. Most Asian markets carry the Szechuan peppercorns (also known as dried Chinese pepper), which are actually not peppercorns at all but the seeds of a prickly ash tree.

¼ tsp	salt	¼ tsp
¾ tsp	Szechuan peppercorns (see page 55)	¾ tsp
3 cloves	garlic, minced	3 cloves
2–3 tbl	minced cilantro (coriander leaves)	2–3 tbl
4 tbl	Chinese sesame paste, drained (see page 55)	4 tbl
4 tsp	sesame oil	4 tsp
3 tbl	soy sauce or tamari	3 tbl
2 tbl	dry sherry	2 tbl
1 tbl	rice vinegar	1 tbl
4 tsp	honey	4 tsp
¼–½ tsp	chile oil	¼–½ tsp

1. In a small frying pan, combine salt and Szechuan peppercorns; cook over medium heat, shaking pan often until salt begins to brown and peppercorns become fragrant, 8–10 minutes.

2. Cool mixture. Grind with mortar and pestle or with spice grinder. Strain mixture to remove hulls.

3. Place salt and Szechuan peppercorn mixture and remaining ingredients in a blender or food processor. Blend until smooth and serve.

Makes ¾ cup (175 ml).

CURRIES AND CURRY PASTES

Although "curry" is often thought of as any dish flavored with curry powder, the term actually refers to a cooking method rather than an ingredient. "To curry" simply means to cook food in a liquid seasoned with a paste of herbs, spices, and aromatic vegetables. Curry pastes can be yellow, green, or red—mild, hot, or incendiary, respectively—depending on the chiles and spices used (see opposite page). They add distinctive flavor to a variety of soups, stews, and stir-fried dishes. Although bottled curry pastes are popular in parts of southeast Asia and elsewhere, many cooks prefer to make their own, selecting ingredients to suit individual tastes, and preparing them just before using.

• Select dried whole ingredients, rather than ground or powdered, whenever possible. Dried whole ingredients can retain their flavor for years but when ground or powdered their flavor and aroma quickly dissipate. When selecting dried ingredients such as galangal or dried Kaffir lime peel (see page 55), pick the largest possible pieces you can find and grind them yourself as needed.

• Keep the curry paste as dry as possible. Curry paste that contains too much liquid causes food to stew rather than fry, lessening the infusion of flavor.

• Curry paste made in a mortar generally does not need liquid added during the pounding process. If you use a blender or food processor, you may have to add oil or coconut milk or cream (whichever the recipe specifies) to blend the mixture thoroughly. If you do add liquid to the curry paste, eliminate or reduce the amount of liquid called for in the recipe and let the paste fry in its own fat.

PREPARING CURRY PASTES

Follow these basic rules for authentic curry:

1. Grind whole spices and dried chiles in an electric spice mill, blender jar, or hand grinder. Soak dried ingredients such as Kaffir lime peel and galangal in warm water to soften.

2. To prepare in a mortar: Start with dried ingredients, adding salt to break down fibers. Finish with softer items such as fresh chiles. Add ground spices last.

3. To prepare in a food processor: Grind or mince harder ingredients by hand. Drop garlic and fresh chiles through the feed tube. Add remaining ingredients and process in pulses, stopping machine frequently to scrape down sides of work bowl. Add oil or coconut milk or cream if necessary to facilitate blending.

4. To prepare in a blender: Use blender accessory jar for blending small amounts. Mince all ingredients first; moisten with oil or coconut milk if necessary.

RED THAI CURRY PASTE

If you use dried Thai chiles, you will probably want to remove the seeds.

7	dried serrano or Thai chiles, finely chopped	7
1 stalk	lemongrass, thinly sliced (see page 55)	1 stalk
2 tbl	minced garlic	2 tbl
¼ cup	minced onion	60 ml
1 tbl	minced coriander root (see page 55)	1 tbl
2 slices	fresh galangal, minced (see page 55)	2 slices
3 strips	Kaffir lime peel, soaked, drained, and minced (see page 55)	3 strips
1 tsp	salt	1 tsp
1 tsp	shrimp paste (see page 55)	1 tsp
2 tsp	ground coriander	2 tsp
½ tsp	ground caraway or cumin	½ tsp

Combine ingredients in a mortar or blender and pound or blend to a paste. Cover and refrigerate until ready to use.

Makes ⅓ cup (85 ml).

GREEN THAI CURRY PASTE

This paste is tame by Thai standards.

3 slices	fresh galangal (see page 55)	3 slices
1 tsp	lime zest	1 tsp
3 tbl	minced coriander root (see page 55)	3 tbl
8	fresh jalapeño or serrano chiles with seeds	8
1 stalk	lemongrass, minced (see page 55)	1 stalk
2 tbl	minced garlic	2 tbl
2 tbl	green onion	2 tbl
1 tsp	shrimp paste (see page 55)	1 tsp
1 tsp	ground coriander	1 tsp
2–3 tbl	oil, for blending (optional)	2–3 tbl

Combine all ingredients in a mortar or blender and pound or blend to a paste, adding oil as necessary. Cover and refrigerate until ready to use.

Makes ⅓ cup (85 ml).

BACKBURNER BARBECUE SAUCE FOR RIBS

This recipe makes enough to prepare 10 pounds (4.6 kg) of back ribs.

14 oz	tomato catsup	400 g
2	onions, chopped	2
2	bell peppers, seeded and chopped	2
12 cloves	garlic, minced	12 cloves
6 small	fresh hot chiles, minced	6 small
1 tbl	crushed dried hot chiles	1 tbl
1 cup	brown sugar	250 ml
½ cup	distilled vinegar	125 ml
1 tbl	mixed dried Italian herbs	1 tbl
1 tsp	liquid smoke flavoring	1 tsp

1. Purée all the sauce ingredients in a blender. Put into a sauce-pan and bring to a boil.

2. Reduce the heat and simmer, stirring frequently, until the sauce is thick and glossy (approximately 15–20 minutes).

3. Use at once or store for up to 3 weeks in the refrigerator, in a jar with a tight-fitting lid.

Makes about 3¾ cups (850 ml).

AGLIO SAUCE

Use this powerfully aromatic Mediterranean sauce to perk up steamed or grilled vegetables.

1 cup (8 oz)	plain yogurt	250 ml (225 g)
15–20 cloves	garlic	15–20 cloves

1. Put the yogurt and garlic in a blender and process until the garlic is totally dissolved.

2. Pour into a serving dish or spoon over vegetables.

Makes about 1½ cups (350 ml).

SAUCE CALIENTE

This peppery, orange-tinted sauce is wonderful with fish or vegetables.

¾ cup	olive oil	175 ml
2 tbl	minced garlic	2 tbl
⅓ tsp	hot-pepper flakes	⅓ tsp
1½ cups	tomato, peeled, seeded, and diced	350 ml
½ cup	soft bread crumbs	125 ml
1½ tsp	chili powder	1½ tsp
2 tsp	anchovy paste	2 tsp
1½ tsp	tomato paste	1½ tsp
2 tsp	sherry vinegar	2 tsp
to taste	salt and freshly ground black pepper	to taste

1. In a medium skillet heat 2 tablespoons of the olive oil over moderate heat. Add garlic, pepper flakes, tomato, and bread crumbs. Sauté 3 minutes. Add chili powder and sauté an additional 2 minutes.

2. Transfer mixture to food processor or blender. Add anchovy paste, tomato paste, and sherry vinegar. Blend until smooth. With motor running, add remaining olive oil very slowly, blending to make a thick sauce.

3. Add salt and pepper to taste and serve.

Makes about 3 cups (700 ml).

Salsa Cruda Zapata

This red table salsa owes its pleasingly chunky texture to fresh ingredients.

1 lb	fresh ripe tomatoes, seeded and diced	450 g
⅓ cup	minced sweet red onion	85 ml
4	fresh jalapeño or serrano chiles, minced	4
¼ cup	minced cilantro (coriander leaves)	60 ml
1 clove	garlic, minced	1 clove
3 tbl	lime juice	3 tbl
to taste	salt and pepper	to taste

1. Combine all ingredients in a small bowl. Taste for seasoning and correct if necessary. Let stand at room temperature (about 30 minutes) to develop flavors.

2. Serve the same day, or tightly cover with plastic wrap and refrigerate for no more than 2 days.

Makes about 3 cups (700 ml).

Salsa Verde Apasionado

Green salsa is good with pork, chicken, and fish dishes. To ease the harsh "bite" of raw garlic, toast the unpeeled garlic cloves on an un-greased skillet until soft. Peel, chop or purée before proceeding.

1–2	fresh or canned jalapeño chiles, chopped	1–2
1 can (12 oz)	tomatillos, drained	1 can (350 g)
2 cloves	garlic, chopped	2 cloves
3 tbl	finely minced white onion	3 tbl
¼ cup	cilantro (coriander leaves), tightly packed	60 ml
¼ tsp	salt	¼ tsp
¼ cup	water	60 ml

1. Place chiles, tomatillos, garlic, onion, cilantro, and salt in a blender or food processor and chop roughly.

2. Add the water in small amounts and blend to the desired consistency.

Makes about 1½ cups (350 ml).

SALSA FRITA

This cooked salsa is fairly hot, but you can make it hotter by increasing the amount of dried hot chiles. Refrigerate the salsa for up to 2 weeks or store it in the freezer for up to 2 months.

2 lb	ripe tomatoes, finely chopped	900 g
8–10	fresh hot chiles, chopped	8–10
3–4 cloves	garlic, chopped	3–4 cloves
2–3	onions, finely chopped	2–3
2 stalks	celery, finely chopped	2 stalks
1 tbl	oil	1 tbl
¼ cup	distilled vinegar	60 ml
2 tbl	sugar	2 tbl
2 tbl	minced cilantro (coriander leaves)	2 tbl
½ tsp	freshly ground black pepper	½ tsp
to taste	salt	to taste
to taste	crushed dried hot chiles	to taste

1. In a blender purée ¼ cup (60 ml) of the chopped tomatoes with as many chiles as can be accommodated. Continue until all chiles have been puréed. Pour purée into a large pot. Add the rest of the tomatoes and remaining ingredients except salt and dried chiles.

2. Cook over high heat for 10 minutes, stirring frequently to avoid scorching. Reduce heat to moderate and cook, stirring occasionally, until salsa is somewhat thickened (about 45 minutes). Season to taste with salt, more sugar or vinegar, and dried chiles. Cook for at least 10 more minutes to incorporate additions.

3. Let cool, spoon into storage containers, and refrigerate or freeze.

Makes about 4 cups (900 ml).

FIRE AND ICE SALSA

Fiery jalapeño makes a stimulating counterpoint to icy melon. Jicama, a round white root with a pleasing crunchy texture, is available at supermarkets and Latin American markets.

1	onion, finely chopped	1
1 tbl	oil	1 tbl
1	jicama, peeled and diced	1
½	cantaloupe, peeled, seeded, and diced	½
½	honeydew, peeled, seeded, and diced	½
⅓ cup	chopped cilantro (coriander leaves)	85 ml
4	fresh red or green jalapeño chiles, minced	4
3 tbl	freshly squeezed lime juice	3 tbl

1. In a small pan sauté onion in oil; let cool.

2. Combine remaining ingredients, stir in sautéed onion, and refrigerate several hours to blend flavors.

Makes 4 cups (900 ml).

SALSA PIÑA

Cilantro, lime juice, and pineapple tantalize the palate with hints of Mexico and Hawaii in every mouthful. Serve with pork, chicken, or duck.

½	fresh pineapple, diced	½
2	fresh tomatoes, diced	2
1	cucumber, seeded and diced	1
2	shallots, minced	2
2	fresh jalapeño chiles, minced	2
¼ cup	minced cilantro (coriander leaves)	60 ml
2 tbl	freshly squeezed lime juice	2 tbl
1 tbl	white wine vinegar	1 tbl
1 tbl	oil	1 tbl
½ tsp	salt	½ tsp

In a 2-quart (1.8-l) bowl stir together all ingredients until well blended. Cover and refrigerate at least 1 hour.

Makes 4 cups (900 ml).

ALLIGATOR PEAR SALSA

Alligator pear—an old name for the avocado—calls to mind the pebbly, rough skin and pear-like shape of the popular Hass variety.

4	tomatoes, peeled, seeded, and chopped	4
3	green onions, minced	3
2–3	fresh serrano chiles, chopped	2–3
1	cucumber, peeled, seeded, and chopped	1
⅓ cup	minced cilantro	85 ml
2	avocados, diced	2
2 tbl	freshly squeezed lime juice	2 tbl
to taste	salt	to taste

1. In a large bowl combine tomatoes, green onions, chiles, cucumber, cilantro, avocados, and lime juice. Stir gently to blend.

2. Season with salt and serve immediately or prepare mixture, without adding salt, up to 1 day ahead. Cover and chill. Add salt just before serving.

Makes about 4 cups (900 ml).

FRESH FRUIT SALSAS

Salsas made with fresh fruit offer the hot tingle of chile and the cool sweetness of ripe fruit. Pineapple, mango, guava, papaya, cantaloupe, honeydew melon, peach, nectarine, plum, or even cranberry—all can make delicious salsas. The subtle flavors of fruit salsas benefit from chilling in the refrigerator for at least an hour or even a day before serving. These salsas have a shorter shelf life than most others and should be used within 2 days.

PICKLED RED HOTS

These pickled chiles will be ready to eat in about three weeks; after that they should be refrigerated. Serve them in burritos or spread on French bread. You'll need a sterilized one-pint jar with a lid and screw top to make these pickles.

2 cups	fresh small hot chiles (see below)	500 ml
6 cloves	garlic	6 cloves
⅓ cup	oil	85 ml
½ tsp	dried dill	½ tsp
½ tsp	sugar	½ tsp
approx. 1½ cups	distilled vinegar	approx. 350 ml

1. With a sharp knife, make a slit in side of each chile. Put chiles into sterilized jar. Add garlic, oil, dill, and sugar.

2. Fill jar with vinegar, put on lid and screw top, and shake to mix. Leave in a cool place until ready to use.

Makes 1 pint (500 ml).

HOT CHILES: HANDLE WITH CARE!

The potency of chiles can be deceptive because of the delayed reaction between contact and sensation. Some people are more sensitive than others to the compound in chiles that can irritate and even burn skin. To prevent painful irritations, follow these precautions when handling chiles:

- *Keep your hands away from your face, especially your eyes, when working with chiles.*

- *After handling chiles, wash hands, utensils, and work surfaces thoroughly with soap and water.*

- *If you plan to handle many chiles or if you have sensitive skin, wear rubber gloves.*

PEPPERY PECANS

Cayenne-coated pecans with a mildly sweet flavor make a spicy cocktail snack or a delicious garnish for a salad. Try using almonds, walnuts, hazelnuts, or a combination. Packaged in fancy tins or jars, these nuts make a fine gift.

4 tbl	unsalted butter	4 tbl
3 tbl	sugar	3 tbl
1½ tbl	salt	1½ tbl
1–2 tsp	cayenne pepper	1–2 tsp
¼ tsp	white pepper	¼ tsp
4 cups	pecan halves	900 ml

1. In a large skillet melt butter and stir in sugar, salt, cayenne, and white pepper; mix well. Add nuts and coat thoroughly. Drain nuts on a tray lined with paper towels.

2. Store in a jar in the refrigerator for up to 2 weeks or place in a plastic freezer bag, press out air, seal tightly, and freeze for up to 2 months.

Makes 4 cups (900 ml).

VINEGARED HORSERADISH

Grate only as much fresh horseradish as you can use right away; leftover horseradish quickly loses its zap.

½ cup	grated fresh horseradish	125 ml
¼ cup	cider vinegar	60 ml
1 tsp	sugar	1 tsp

In a blender purée all ingredients until smooth. For a thinner mixture, add more vinegar, 1 teaspoon at a time. Add more sugar to taste and serve.

Makes about ½ cup (125 ml).

CHEDDAR-HORSERADISH SAUCE

English cooking often uses both mustard and horseradish to create zesty sauces.

2 tbl	butter	2 tbl
2 tbl	unbleached flour	2 tbl
1 tsp	dry mustard	1 tsp
2 cups	milk	500 ml
2	eggs, well beaten	2
1 cup	shredded sharp Cheddar cheese	250 ml
3 tbl	prepared horseradish (see page 65)	3 tbl
½ tsp	dried dill	½ tsp
1 tsp	chopped canned pimento	1 tsp
to taste	salt	to taste

1. Melt butter in a saucepan over medium heat. Add flour and mustard and stir briskly until a paste forms. Add the milk in a thin stream, whisking all the while, until the mixture is smooth and thickened.

2. Pour half of the mixture into a small bowl and whisk to cool. Whisking all the while, slowly pour the beaten eggs into the white sauce, then slowly pour the egg mixture back into the white sauce, whisking constantly until thickened, (about 10–15 minutes).

3. When thickened, smooth, and glossy, add the remaining ingredients, stir to blend, and adjust seasoning. Add more horseradish if desired. Serve warm.

Makes about 4 cups (900 ml).

FIREHOUSE MUSTARD

This British-inspired recipe is particularly good with roast beef or ham.

3 tbl	dry mustard	3 tbl
½ tsp	cayenne pepper	½ tsp
½ tsp	grated fresh ginger	½ tsp
1 tbl	dark brown sugar	1 tbl
¼ cup	cider vinegar	60 ml

In a bowl mix together mustard, cayenne, ginger, and sugar. Gradually add cider vinegar, stirring constantly until mustard is the desired consistency.

Makes about ¼ cup (60 ml).

DIM SUM DIPPING MUSTARD

Excellent as a condiment for the delightful tidbits that make up traditional dim sum, this Asian-style mustard can complement foods of just about any origin.

⅓ cup	soy sauce or tamari	85 ml
1 tbl	grated fresh ginger	1 tbl
2 tbl	dry mustard	2 tbl
2 tbl	sugar	2 tbl
6 cloves	garlic	6 cloves
¼ tsp	coarsely ground black pepper	¼ tsp

1. In a blender purée all ingredients except black pepper until liquified. Strain.

2. Add pepper and stir. Serve at once or refrigerate in a covered jar for up to 2 weeks.

Makes about ⅓ cup (85 ml).

FIRE STARTERS: SOUPS AND SALADS

A blistering bowl of soup or a cool salad with a snappy come-back—either makes a welcome alternative to luke-warm menu openers. In the following pages you'll discover soups and salads from China, Japan, Southeast Asia, and Mexico, all of them designed to fire up your appetite and get a good meal off to a great start.

INDONESIAN CHILIED CHICKEN SOUP

Definitely not the chicken soup your mother made to soothe the sniffles, this version gains extra heat from the sambal (hot chile sauce) stirred in just before eating.

1	chicken, about 4 lb (1.8 kg), cut up	1
1	onion, diced	1
2 tbl each	minced ginger and garlic	2 tbl each
1 stalk	lemongrass, sliced (see page 55)	1 stalk
2 tsp	ground coriander	2 tsp
1 tsp	ground cumin	1 tsp
1½ tsp	freshly ground black pepper	1½ tsp
1½ tsp	galangal (see page 55)	1½ tsp
1 tsp	sugar	1 tsp
1 cup	shredded cabbage or Chinese cabbage	1 cup
¼ lb	bean thread noodles, soaked in hot water until soft	115 g
1 cup	diced red bell pepper	250 ml
to taste	salt	to taste
1 recipe	Sambal Bajak (see page 13)	1 recipe

1. In a large saucepan cover chicken with cold water and bring to a boil. Reduce heat slightly and cook 5 minutes, skimming foam from the surface. Add onion, ginger, garlic, lemongrass, coriander, cumin, black pepper, galangal, and sugar. Simmer until chicken is tender (about 45 minutes).

2. When chicken is done, remove from soup and let cool. Bone and shred meat, and place in the middle of a platter.

3. Blanch cabbage in boiling water for 30 seconds, drain, and transfer to platter. Drain bean threads, and place on platter. Arrange bell pepper on platter.

4. Skim fat from soup, salt to taste, and strain. For each serving, combine some chicken, bean threads, cabbage, and peppers in a bowl and ladle in the hot soup. Add sambal to taste.

Serves 4 to 6.

HOT AND SOUR THAI SOUP

This soup can be hot or incendiary, depending upon the amount of chile used. For more heat, mince some of the chiles and pound them in with the seasoning paste.

1 stalk	lemongrass (see page 55)	1 stalk
1 qt	water or chicken stock	900 ml
1 tbl	minced coriander root (see page 55)	1 tbl
½ tsp	peppercorns	½ tsp
2 cloves	garlic, peeled	2 cloves
3 tbl	freshly squeezed lime juice	3 tbl
1–2	fresh hot chiles, loose seeds removed	1–2
2	Kaffir lime leaves (see page 55)	2
1 lb	shrimp, peeled and deveined	450 g
1 cup	sliced mushrooms	250 ml
to taste	fish sauce (see page 55)	to taste
as needed	sliced green onions, for garnish	as needed

1. Cut top of lemongrass stalk into 2-inch (5-cm) sections, pound lightly with side of knife blade, and simmer in stock 15 minutes. Slice remaining lemongrass as finely as possible.

2. In a mortar or blender, combine sliced lemongrass, coriander root, peppercorns, and garlic and pound or blend to a paste. Moisten with a little lime juice if necessary.

3. Strain stock and discard lemongrass. Return stock to pan and add paste, chiles, lime leaves, and remaining lime juice. Simmer 5 minutes, add shrimp and mushrooms, and simmer until shrimp turns pink and opaque. Season to taste with fish sauce and garnish with green onions.

Serves 4 to 6.

UDON WITH CHILES IN BROTH

For a blistering bowlful, add black and cayenne pepper to this Japanese peasant dish of noodles and broth. Udon noodles, dried bonita flakes, and nori seaweed are available in Asian markets.

3	shiitake mushrooms	3
6 cups	chicken stock	1.4 l
2 tbl	dried bonita flakes	2 tbl
6 cloves	garlic, crushed	6 cloves
1	onion, quartered	1
1 tbl	chopped fresh ginger	1 tbl
2 tbl	crushed dried chiles	2 tbl
1 tbl	sugar	1 tbl
3 sheets	nori seaweed	3 sheets
to taste	salt and freshly ground pepper	to taste
14 oz	udon noodles, cooked and drained	400 g
as needed	oil, for coating pan	as needed
2	eggs, lightly beaten	2
3	green onions, finely chopped	3
2 small	fresh hot chiles, seeded and minced	2 small
8 oz	tofu, cubed	225 g
12	snow peas, stemmed and cut into slivers	12

1. Soak mushrooms in warm water to cover for 1 hour. Drain and set aside.

2. In a large pot, put stock, bonita flakes, garlic, onion, ginger, dried chiles, sugar, and nori, and bring to a boil. Reduce heat to low and cook for 45 minutes. Season to taste with salt, pepper, and more dried chiles. Cook for another 10 minutes.

3. Strain stock, return to pot, bring to a boil, and add cooked noodles. Reduce heat and simmer for 5 minutes. Cut mushrooms into quarters. In a lightly oiled pan, scramble eggs until firm. Remove eggs from pan and sliver finely. Add eggs and remaining ingredients to noodles and stock. Stir gently and simmer for another minute before serving.

Serves 4 to 6.

Yucatán Chile-Citrus Soup

To approximate the taste of the sour lemon, a fruit that is native to the Yucatán, some Mexican recipes for this dish suggest using a combination of lime and lemon or adding grapefruit zest. Whichever citrus you use, the result is a spicy soup with a refreshing flavor.

1 tbl	oil	1 tbl
½	onion, chopped	½
2	fresh jalapeño chiles, seeded, deveined, and minced	2
2	tomatoes, peeled and chopped	2
8 cups	chicken broth	1.8 l
1	onion, quartered	1
3 cloves	garlic, coarsely chopped	3 cloves
6	peppercorns	6
½ tsp	thyme	½ tsp
1 tsp	salt	1 tsp
6	limes	6
2 cups	shredded chicken	500 ml
⅓ cup	chopped cilantro (coriander leaves)	85 ml
2	avocados, sliced	2
as needed	tortilla chips	as needed

1. In soup pot, heat the oil and sauté the chopped onion and chiles over medium heat. Cook until the onion is soft. Add the tomatoes and cook until soft.

2. Add the broth to the soup pot with the quartered onion, garlic, peppercorns, thyme, and salt, and bring to a boil. Reduce heat and add the juice of 3 or 4 of the limes, plus a lime half. Simmer 30 minutes.

3. Remove the lime half, add the shredded chicken, and simmer 20 minutes. Stir in the cilantro.

4. Ladle the soup into serving bowls. Garnish with avocado slices and lime wedges cut from the remaining limes. Serve with tortilla chips.

Serves 8.

ENSENADA ENSALADA

You can make this a day ahead of serving.

2 cups	corn kernels, cooked	500 ml
2 cans (15 oz each)	black beans	2 cans (430 g each)
1	red bell pepper, diced	1
1	red onion, minced	1
2–4	fresh jalapeño chiles, minced	2–4
1 clove	garlic, minced	1 clove
1 bunch	cilantro (coriander leaves), minced	1 bunch
1	lime, juiced	1
1 tsp	salt	1 tsp
1 tsp	freshly ground black pepper	1 tsp
5 tbl	oil	5 tbl
5 tbl	red wine vinegar	5 tbl

In a 3-quart (2.7-l) bowl combine all ingredients. Chill for 1–24 hours. Taste for seasoning before serving.

Serves 8.

SZECHUAN SPROUT SALAD

Control the heat by adjusting the amount of hot-pepper flakes you add.

½ lb	fresh bean sprouts	225 g
2 tbl	rice wine vinegar	2 tbl
1 tbl	soy sauce or tamari	1 tbl
2 tsp	sesame oil	2 tsp
½ tsp	sugar	½ tsp
⅛–¼ tsp	crushed hot-pepper flakes	⅛–¼ tsp
3 tbl	thinly sliced green onion	3 tbl

Rinse sprouts and pat dry with paper towels. In a small bowl stir together vinegar, soy sauce, sesame oil, sugar, and hot-pepper flakes. Place sprouts and onion in serving bowl, add dressing, and toss to coat. Serve at once or refrigerate for up to 4 hours.

Serves 4.

ASPARAGUS SALAD CHINOIS

This spicy salad has a cooling effect and works well with any Chinese menu. Adjust the spiciness to your taste by increasing or decreasing the amounts of cayenne pepper, garlic, and ginger.

1 lb	asparagus	450 g
1 tbl	minced garlic	1 tbl
1 tbl	grated ginger	1 tbl
½ tsp	salt	½ tsp
½ tsp	honey	½ tsp
2 tbl	soy sauce or tamari	2 tbl
1 tsp	Asian sesame oil (see page 55)	1 tsp
1 tbl	rice vinegar	1 tbl
¼ tsp	cayenne pepper	¼ tsp
½ tsp	hot-pepper flakes	½ tsp

1. Trim ends of asparagus and slice each stalk diagonally into 3-inch (7.5-cm) pieces. Steam until tender (8–10 minutes). Drain and set aside.

2. In a large bowl combine remaining ingredients. Toss with asparagus. Chill before serving.

Serves 4.

PREPARING GRATED GINGER

In much of Asian cooking, fresh ginger figures in a variety of dishes from salads to sweets. Choose crisp knobs that snap easily into pieces and store them for up to 2–3 weeks in the crisper or in a plastic bag with a bit of paper towel to absorb moisture. To grate, use a special porcelain or bamboo ginger grater to rake the flesh off the root fibers. A conventional metal box grater will do the job but is difficult to clean.

Hunan Soba-Seafood Salad

If you like spicy salads, you'll make this one time and again. For extra flavor, marinate the seafood and noodles in the spicy sauce for an hour, then toss with greens before serving warm or chilled. Soba, thick noodles made from buckwheat, are available in supermarkets or Asian markets.

1 cup	white wine	250 ml
¼ lb	medium prawns, peeled	115 g
¼ lb	scallops	115 g
6	mussels in shell, scrubbed well	6
4 tsp	finely minced garlic	4 tsp
½ cup	minced green onions	125 ml
2 tsp	cayenne pepper or hot-pepper flakes	2 tsp
4 tsp	tahini (sesame butter)	4 tsp
1 tsp	Asian sesame oil (see page 55)	1 tsp
2 tbl	soy sauce or tamari	2 tbl
½ tsp	honey	½ tsp
1 tsp	grated ginger	1 tsp
10 oz	soba noodles, cooked	285 g
as needed	lettuce, for lining platter	as needed
½ cup	cucumbers, peeled, halved, and sliced	125 ml
½ cup	sliced red bell pepper	125 ml

1. In a saucepan over medium-high heat, bring wine to boil. Add prawns, scallops, and mussels in shell, cover, and cook 2 minutes. Drain seafood and rinse under cold water. Remove mussels from shell and set seafood aside.

2. In large bowl mix together garlic, green onions, cayenne, tahini, sesame oil, soy sauce, honey, and ginger. Add noodles and seafood and mix well. Let chill for 30 minutes, if desired.

3. To serve, line a large platter with lettuce. Place noodles in center. Arrange cucumbers and red bell pepper around noodles and serve.

Serves 6.

FIRE-EATER'S FEAST: ENTRÉES AND ACCOMPANIMENTS

Eating fire has its rewards, and a number of them are presented in the section that follows. From Southeast Asia to the United Kingdom, from the Caribbean to Mexico and the U.S.A., most all the cuisines that both fuel and satisfy the craving for ever-hotter edibles are represented here. Providing you can take the heat, you'll find enough main courses and side dishes to fuel a month-long feast.

KOREAN BULGOKI

Salty, spicy, grilled Korean short ribs have attained worldwide popularity in recent years.

¾ cup	soy sauce or tamari	175 ml
1 cup	dry sherry	250 ml
1 tsp	Asian sesame oil (see page 55)	1 tsp
2–3	fresh jalapeño or serrano chiles, sliced	2–3
1 tsp	freshly ground black pepper	1 tsp
5	green onions, including green tops, thinly sliced	5
1 tbl	minced garlic	1 tbl
¼ cup	slivered fresh ginger	60 ml
4 lb	meaty short ribs, thickly cut	1.8 kg
¼ cup	sesame seed	60 ml
2 tbl	minced cilantro (coriander leaves)	2 tbl
as needed	steamed rice, for accompaniment	as needed

1. Mix soy sauce, sherry, oil, chiles, black pepper, green onions, garlic, and ginger in large roasting pan. Add ribs, turning them several times in liquid. Cover pan and let ribs marinate 3 hours at room temperature or overnight in the refrigerator, turning several times to coat meat thoroughly.

2. Preheat oven to 375°F (190°C). Remove ribs from marinade, reserving marinade. Return ribs to pan, bone side down. Bake until tender (about 40 minutes–1 hour), depending on thickness, brushing with reserved marinade every 10 minutes.

3. At the final basting, sprinkle ribs with sesame seed. When done remove from oven, sprinkle with cilantro to taste, and serve immediately with steamed rice.

Serves 3 or 4.

KUNG PAO SHRIMP WITH CASHEWS

This variation on a Szechuan classic uses cashews and shrimp instead of peanuts and chicken. When charring the chiles, don't breathe the strong chile fumes.

1 cup	jumbo raw cashews	250 ml
1½ tbl	soy sauce	1½ tbl
2 tbl	red wine vinegar	2 tbl
2 tsp	sugar	2 tsp
1 tsp	Asian sesame oil (see page 55)	1 tsp
2 tbl	peanut oil	2 tbl
½ tsp	salt	½ tsp
8 small	dried red chiles	8 small
2 tsp	minced fresh ginger	2 tsp
2 cloves	garlic, minced	2 cloves
1	green or red bell pepper, seeded and cut into 1-inch (2.5-cm) squares	1
1 lb	medium shrimp, shelled, deveined, and patted dry	450 g

1. Preheat oven to 325°F (160°C). In a flat pan spread cashews in a single layer; roast until golden brown (about 10 minutes), stirring occasionally. Remove and set aside.

2. In a small bowl combine soy sauce, vinegar, sugar, and sesame oil; set aside.

3. Preheat wok over medium heat until hot, then pour in peanut oil. Add salt and chiles; cook until chiles are charred (about 15 seconds). Add ginger and garlic; stir-fry until fragrant and lightly browned (about 30 seconds).

4. Increase heat to high; add bell pepper and stir-fry until pepper is seared (about 30 seconds). Add shrimp a handful at a time and stir-fry until shrimp are pink and firm (about 2 minutes total). Add reserved sauce mixture; toss and stir until sauce thickens to a glaze (about 30 seconds). Remove from heat. Gently stir in roasted cashews. Serve hot.

Serves 4.

STORING AND PRESERVING CHILES

The availability of good fresh chiles varies somewhat seasonally. Stock up whenever the supply is abundant and you'll never be caught without this prime heat source.

To Refrigerate Fresh Chiles *Store loosely wrapped in refrigerator. Poblano, Anaheim, New Mexico, and other mild chiles will keep 3–7 days; jalapeños and most other hot chiles will keep for up to 3 weeks.*

To Freeze Fresh Chiles *Before freezing mild chiles, roast and peel them (see Preparing Roasted Chiles on page 79). When chiles are cool, seed and devein them. Wrap each chile in plastic wrap or waxed paper, then pack individually wrapped chiles in a large plastic bag and seal tightly. Before freezing small hot chiles, cook them for 1–2 minutes in a dry skillet or boil them 1–2 minutes in a small amount of water.*

To Dry Fresh Chiles *Green and red Anaheim chiles and yellow, green, or orange jalapeños are the best for drying.*

To dry indoors: Use a large needle threaded with nylon thread. Push the needle through the stems, positioning chiles alternately to the left and right. Tie a loop at the top of the thread and hang chiles in an attic or other warm, dry place for about 3 weeks, until they shrivel and feel dry. If the air becomes humid and chiles start to mold, complete the drying process in an oven or dehydrator.

To dry in an oven, dehydrator, or the sun: Let whole, halved, or sliced chiles dry for 2–5 hours in a 140°F (60°C) oven or for 12–18 hours in a dehydrator set at 120°F (49°C). Whole chiles threaded on a string will dry in 1–2 days in the sunshine.

To Store Dried Chiles *Dried chiles (packed whole or ground) in tightly sealed jars will keep 3–4 months under cool, dry conditions. If condensation appears in jars (a sign that chiles are not fully dried), freeze or use chiles at once. For longer storage, pack whole or ground dried chiles in plastic bags, seal tightly, and store in the freezer.*

WOKKED CHICKEN HUNAN

This sizzling Far East specialty cooks in less than 10 minutes. Serve with a cucumber salad and steamed asparagus for a simple but impressive presentation (see photo on page 10).

12–15	dried small hot chiles	12–15
1 tsp	oil	1 tsp
⅓ cup	sliced green onion	85 ml
⅓ cup	sliced carrot	85 ml
⅓ cup	sliced red bell pepper	85 ml
⅓ cup	broccoli florets	85 ml
¼ cup	dry sherry	60 ml
2 cups	shredded cooked chicken breast	500 ml
1 tsp	Asian sesame oil (see page 55)	1 tsp
2 tsp	minced garlic	2 tsp
2 tsp	sesame paste (see page 55)	2 tsp
1 tbl	rice vinegar	1 tbl
2 tbl	soy sauce or tamari	2 tbl
1 tsp	honey	1 tsp
1 tbl	chile paste with garlic (see page 55)	1 tbl
2 tsp	grated fresh ginger	2 tsp

1. Stem chiles and remove seeds. Put chiles in a small bowl and cover with boiling water. Let sit until water cools. Drain and mince chiles.

2. In a wok or skillet, heat oil and sauté green onion until soft but not browned. Add carrot, bell pepper, broccoli, chiles, and sherry. Cook rapidly over high heat, covered, for 3 minutes.

3. Add remaining ingredients. Lower heat and cook, covered, for 5 minutes, stirring frequently. Serve hot.

Serves 6.

CHICKEN TANGERINE

Turn up the heat in this Chinese dish by adding more hot-pepper flakes.

1	egg white	1
3 tbl	dry sherry	3 tbl
2 tbl	cornstarch	2 tbl
1 lb	boneless skinned chicken, diced	450 g
½ cup	thinly sliced green onion	125 ml
2 tbl	minced fresh ginger	2 tbl
2 tbl	minced garlic	2 tbl
1 tbl	tangerine zest	1 tbl
½–1 tsp	hot-pepper flakes	½–1 tsp
½ cup + 2 tbl	chicken stock	125 ml + 2tbl
2 tbl	soy sauce or tamari	2 tbl
2 tbl	rice wine vinegar	2 tbl
2 tbl	sugar	2 tbl
⅓ cup	oil	85 ml

1. In a small bowl whisk egg white and 1 tablespoon each of the sherry and cornstarch. Pour over chicken and refrigerate at least 8 hours. In a bowl combine green onion, ginger, garlic, tangerine zest, and hot-pepper flakes and set aside. In another bowl combine the ½ cup stock, soy sauce, remaining sherry, vinegar, and sugar. Stir to dissolve and set aside.

2. Preheat wok over high heat. Remove chicken from marinade; discard marinade. Swirl 3 tablespoons of the oil around wok, add chicken, and stir-fry until partially cooked (1-2 minutes). Remove and set aside. Make a paste of the remaining cornstarch and chicken stock and set aside.

3. Heat remaining oil in wok. Add onion-ginger-garlic mixture and stir-fry over medium-high heat until fragrant. Add chicken-stock mixture and simmer, stirring frequently, until heated through (about 2 minutes). Add chicken and cook until firm (about 4 minutes). Reduce heat to low. Mix in cornstarch mixture and stir until sauce is glossy. Serve immediately.

Serves 4.

LEMONGRASS CHICKEN

Lemongrass flakes or powder won't work for this dish; if you can't find fresh lemongrass, just leave it out and enjoy the flavor of the fresh chiles and basil.

2 stalks	lemongrass (see page 55)	2 stalks
1 lb	bonelesss chicken breast, cut into strips	450 g
2 tbl	fish sauce (see page 55)	2 tbl
1 tsp	sugar	1 tsp
½ tsp	salt	½ tsp
¼ tsp	freshly ground black pepper	¼ tsp
3	green onions, cut into 1-inch (2.5-cm) pieces	3
1 tbl	minced garlic	1 tbl
as needed	oil, for stir-frying	as needed
2	fresh red chiles, seeded and julienned	2
1 handful	chopped fresh basil or mint leaves, or a combination	1 handful

1. Remove tops and tough outer leaves of lemongrass and slice tender hearts as thin as possible. In a bowl combine chicken, lemongrass, 1 tablespoon of the fish sauce, sugar, salt, pepper, green onions, and garlic. Toss to coat chicken evenly and allow to marinate ½–1 hour.

2. In a wok or skillet heat oil over medium-high heat. Add chiles, stir-fry a few seconds, and add chicken mixture. Stir-fry until chicken shows no trace of pink (about 3–4 minutes). Add a little water if necessary to prevent scorching. When chicken is done to taste sprinkle with remaining fish sauce, toss with basil or mint, and transfer to serving platter.

Serves 4 with other dishes.

Malaysian Calamari

This fiery Southeast Asian delicacy takes your breath away, so serve it in very small amounts, as a condiment with steamed or grilled fish. Mild-flavored calamari (squid) is the perfect foil for the chiles.

½ cup	diced onion	125 ml
2 cloves	garlic, minced	2 cloves
3–4	fresh hot red chiles, minced	3–4
	or	
1 tsp	Sambal Ulek (see page 14)	1 tsp
½ tsp	salt	½ tsp
2 tbl	oil	2 tbl
as needed	paprika	as needed
½ lb	calamari (squid), cleaned, skinned and cut in rings	225 g
2 tbl	lemon juice	2 tbl

1. To prepare in a mortar, pound onion, garlic, chiles, and salt together to a coarse paste. To prepare in a blender or food processor, grind together with oil.

2. In a wok or skillet, heat oil over low heat and add paste. (If oil was used in grinding paste, add paste to dry wok.) Cook slowly until quite fragrant and oil is well stained with red. Add paprika as needed to enhance color.

3. Turn heat to medium-high, add squid and lemon juice, and cook just until squid is done (about 2 minutes). Serve hot or at room temperature.

Serves 4 to 6 with other dishes.

A TASTE OF ASIA

Authentic ingredients make all the difference in the flavor of Asian dishes. Most supermarkets stock soy sauce and other common Asian staples, but for the following ingredients you may need to shop at an Asian market. Alternatives are given if a substitute is available.

Asian sesame oil *Also called dark sesame oil; an aromatic, amber-colored oil used most often for flavoring rather than cooking.*

Chile paste with garlic *Best sautéed in oil a few seconds before mixing in with other ingredients. Substitute: ¼ teaspoon cayenne pepper for 1 tablespoon of chile paste.*

Coriander root *The root portion of cilantro (fresh coriander).*

Fish sauce *A salty, brown liquid with a pungent odor that dissipates during cooking; the Southeast Asian equivalent of soy sauce.*

Galangal *A relative of ginger with mustard-like overtones; available fresh or dried. Dried galangal should be soaked in water until soft and pliable.*

Kaffir lime leaves *Aromatic, lime-flavored leaves; available fresh or dried. Substitute: lime zest.*

Lemongrass *Also known as citronella; a grassy plant with a lemony aroma; available fresh or dried. Substitute: the zest of half a lemon for 1 stalk of lemongrass.*

Rice wine vinegar *A dark brown, richly flavored vinegar made from rice wine. Substitute: balsamic vinegar.*

Salam leaf or curry leaf *Two similar ingredients that often can be substituted for one another. Salam, or Indonesian bay leaf, has a tea-like flavor and aroma; curry leaf has a mild sweet-spicy aroma; available fresh or dried.*

Sesame paste *A flavorful "butter" made from roasted sesame seeds. Substitute: peanut butter.*

Shrimp paste *A brownish paste made from fermented shrimp; available fresh or dried. Substitute: anchovy paste.*

CURRIED SHRIMP SATÉ

Shrimp paste gives this dish authentic flavor, but be sure to mix it thoroughly into the marinade. If any lumps remain, they will taste unpleasantly strong.

4 cloves	garlic, minced	4 cloves
¼ tsp	shrimp paste (see page 55)	¼ tsp
¼ tsp	Sambal Ulek (see page 14)	¼ tsp
1 tbl	oil	1 tbl
⅓ cup	thick coconut milk (see page 58)	85 ml
1 tbl	lemon or lime juice	1 tbl
1 tsp	lemon or lime zest	1 tsp
½ tsp	salt	½ tsp
1 lb	medium-large shrimp, peeled and deveined	450 g
as needed	skewers	as needed

1. Pound garlic, shrimp paste, and Sambal Ulek together in a mortar, mixing thoroughly.

2. In a small skillet heat oil over medium heat. Add garlic mixture and cook until the smell of the shrimp paste dissipates. Remove from heat and stir in coconut milk, lemon juice, lemon zest, and salt. Allow to cool.

3. Thread shrimp onto skewers. Rub coconut mixture over shrimp and marinate 1–3 hours.

4. Grill shrimp over a medium-hot fire until they are opaque. Turn once during cooking and spread with any remaining marinade. Serve hot.

Serves 4.

Indonesian Crab Curry

This light version of curry features nonfat milk and grated coconut.

1½ tsp	cayenne pepper	1½ tsp
1 tsp	grated fresh ginger	1 tsp
½ tsp	freshly ground black pepper	½ tsp
4 cloves	garlic, minced	4 cloves
5	shallots, minced	5
⅓ cup	chopped cilantro (coriander leaves)	85 ml
½ tsp	lime zest	½ tsp
½ tsp	salt	½ tsp
1 tsp	shrimp paste (see page 55)	1 tsp
½ cup	grated coconut	125 ml
2 cups	nonfat milk	500 ml
2 tbl	soy sauce or tamari	2 tbl
1 tbl	honey	1 tbl
1 lb	cooked crabmeat	450 g
5 cups	cooked rice	1.1 l

1. In a stockpot combine cayenne, ginger, pepper, garlic, shallots, cilantro, lime zest, salt, shrimp paste, coconut, and milk. Bring to a boil and cook over medium-high heat for 10 minutes.

2. Add soy sauce, honey, and crabmeat. Heat through and serve.

Serves 6.

Coconut Milk for Curries

Thai curries frequently call for coconut milk, made by steeping grated coconut flesh, then straining and pressing it through cheesecloth. Like dairy milk, coconut milk (available canned in larger supermarkets and Asian markets) can vary in fat content. If a recipe specifies "thick" milk, use canned coconut milk and shake the can before opening to "homogenize" it. For "medium" coconut milk, skim the coconut cream, the thick white substance that rises to the top of the can, before pouring the milk from the can. Coconut cream can replace the oil in most curry recipes.

GOLDEN TRIANGLE BRAISED CHICKEN

This dish combines the Laotian technique of steaming chicken in leaves with the flavor of Thai curry. The banana-leaf wrappers impart a subtle fragrance to this hybrid dish but are not eaten. Frozen banana leaves, available at Asian markets, keep well after thawing. Substitute aluminum foil for the leaves as a last resort.

as needed	banana leaves, cut into 12-inch (30-cm) squares,	as needed
	or	
	12-inch (30-cm) squares of aluminum foil	
2 lb	chicken parts, cut into pieces for braising	900 g
1 tbl	fish sauce (see page 55)	1 tbl
½ cup	thick coconut milk (see page 58)	125 ml
1–2 tbl	Red Thai Curry Paste (see page 19)	1–2 tbl
as needed	Kaffir lime leaves (see page 55)	as needed

1. Pour hot water over banana leaves to soften them; drain and set aside.

2. Sprinkle chicken pieces with fish sauce and let stand 5 minutes. In a wok or skillet, heat coconut milk and curry paste over low heat until mixture begins to bubble. Remove from heat and allow to cool.

3. Toss chicken pieces in curry mixture to coat. Place 1 or more pieces in the middle of a square of banana leaf, add a spoonful of the curry mixture, and top with a lime leaf. Carefully fold banana leaf into a rectangular package, securing the ends with a toothpick or tying them with string. The leaves split easily, so start with more than you think you will need and handle them carefully. Place in steamer, seam side up, and steam 45 minutes.

Serves 4 with other dishes.

CURRIED SHRIMP CILANTRO

A Thai green curry, such as this one made with shrimp, is incomplete without fresh herbs—basil, mint, or cilantro.

2 cups	thick coconut milk (see page 58)	500 ml
¼ cup	coconut cream (see page 58)	60 ml
2 tbl	Green Thai Curry Paste (see page 19)	2 tbl
1 cup	diced new potatoes	250 ml
1 lb	shrimp, peeled and deveined	450 g
½ cup	water	125 ml
3	Kaffir lime leaves (see page 55)	3
2 tsp	fish sauce (see page 55)	2 tsp
1 cup	peeled, seeded, and chopped tomatoes	250 ml
½ cup	cilantro (coriander leaves)	125 ml

1. Heat wok over medium-high heat. Skim coconut cream from coconut milk and spoon into heated wok. Set coconut milk aside. Add curry paste to wok and cook on high heat until oil begins to separate.

2. Reduce heat to medium and add potatoes. Cook, stirring, until potatoes are nearly done. Add shrimp, coconut milk, water, and lime leaves.

3. Bring to a boil and cook until shrimp and potatoes are done. If sauce thickens too quickly, thin with a little more water. Season to taste with fish sauce and stir in tomatoes and cilantro.

Serves 4 with other dishes.

TANDOORI TURKEY

This Indian-style dish (traditionally made with cut-up chicken, as in the photo on the opposite page) makes great salads and sandwiches, so plan to make extra for leftovers.

2 tsp	cumin seed	2 tsp
1 tsp	whole coriander, crushed	1 tsp
¼ tsp	saffron threads	¼ tsp
2 tbl	boiling water	2 tbl
1 tsp	turmeric	1 tsp
2	shallots, minced	2
3 cloves	garlic, minced	3 cloves
1 tsp	minced fresh ginger	1 tsp
¼ cup	minced cilantro (coriander leaves)	60 ml
1	jalapeño chile, minced	1
1 tbl	paprika	1 tbl
¼ tsp	cayenne pepper	¼ tsp
1 tsp	salt	1 tsp
1 cup	yogurt	250 ml
3 tbl	freshly squeezed lemon juice	3 tbl
6 tbl	unsalted butter, melted	6 tbl
4	turkey fillets, halved lengthwise	4

1. In a dry skillet over medium heat, toast cumin seed and coriander until barely browned (4–5 minutes). In a 1-quart (900 ml) bowl stir together saffron and the boiling water.

2. Into the saffron liquid stir cumin seed, coriander, turmeric, shallots, garlic, ginger, cilantro, chile, paprika, cayenne, salt, yogurt, lemon juice, and 3 tablespoons melted butter. Mix thoroughly. Rub this marinade into turkey; let marinate in refrigerator for 2 hours, or overnight.

3. Preheat oven to 500°F (260°C). Place turkey fillets on a broiler rack in a shallow pan and roast for 4–5 minutes. Turn, baste with remaining melted butter, and roast 3–5 minutes, depending on size and thickness of fillets, until done to taste.

Serves 8.

YORKSHIRE HOT POT

Serve this lamb and oyster stew with horseradish and hot brown mustard.

¼ cup	unbleached flour	60 ml
1¼ tsp	salt	1¼ tsp
2–3 tsp	coarsely ground black pepper	2–3 tsp
1–2 tsp	dry mustard	1–2 tsp
3 tbl	paprika	3 tbl
2 lb	lean lamb, cut into bite-sized pieces	900 g
6–8	lamb kidneys, halved lengthwise	6–8
3 tbl	oil	3 tbl
1	onion, chopped	1
2 cups	beef stock	500 ml
1 scant tsp	sugar	1 scant tsp
¼ tsp	dried thyme	¼ tsp
4	potatoes, peeled and thinly sliced	4
2 pt	bottled oysters, drained	900 ml
12	small boiling onions, peeled	12
1 lb	button mushrooms, quartered	450 g

1. Combine flour, 1 teaspoon of the salt, 1½–2½ teaspoons of the pepper, mustard, and paprika in a bowl. Add lamb and kidneys and coat each piece. Shake off excess flour.

2. In a heavy skillet over high heat, heat oil and brown lamb and kidneys on all sides. Remove meats and set aside. Sauté onion in oil remaining in skillet and then add stock, sugar, thyme, and the remaining salt and pepper. Reduce heat to medium and cook, stirring, for about 2 minutes. Remove from heat.

3. Preheat oven to 350°F (175°C). Place half the potato slices on the bottom of a 5-quart (4.5 l) casserole with a tight-fitting lid. Add lamb, kidneys, oysters, boiling onions, and mushrooms in layers and top with remaining potatoes. Pour in stock. Sprinkle cheese, bread crumbs, and parsley over top. Cover and bake until meat is very tender (about 1½ hours). Remove lid during last 15 minutes to brown.

Serves 6 to 8.

BEEF CORNUCOPIAS WITH HORSERADISH FILLING

This British favorite makes a hearty appetizer or main dish for a buffet supper.

4 oz	cream cheese, softened	115 g
¼–⅓ cup	prepared or fresh horseradish	60–85 ml
2 tbl	minced fresh chives	2 tbl
1 tbl	minced red bell pepper	1 tbl
2 cloves	garlic, minced	2 cloves
½ tsp	dried dill	½ tsp
1 tbl	chopped ripe olives	1 tbl
⅓ cup	minced red onion	85 ml
¼ tsp	coarsely ground black pepper	¼ tsp
to taste	salt	to taste
24 thin slices	medium-rare roast beef	24 thin slices
as needed	watercress sprigs, for garnish	as needed

1. Put all of the ingredients except the beef and watercress in a bowl and blend well with a fork. Spread each slice of beef with the cheese-horseradish mixture.

2. Roll each slice firmly into a cone and secure with a cocktail pick. Place a tuft of watercress in open end of each cone and arrange on a serving platter. Chill before serving.

Makes 24.

TAMING THE WILD HORSERADISH

The pungency of horseradish, especially when it's freshly grated, can be startling to the uninitiated. Prepared (bottled) horseradish is slightly more tame than the fresh root, which grows wild over much of Europe and Asia. If you want to substitute the freshly grated root in a recipe that calls for prepared horseradish, start out with about half the amount called for in the recipe. Add more if you dare.

Jamaican "Jerked" Pork

The seasoning mixture gives oven-roasted pork loin a "jerked" flavor.

6–8 lb	pork loin roast	2.8–3.6 kg
2 cups	chicken stock	500 ml
1 cup	dark brown sugar	250 ml
15–20	scallions	15–20
10–15 cloves	garlic, minced	10–15 cloves
½ tbl	grated fresh ginger	½ tbl
⅛ tsp	ground cloves	⅛ tsp
2 tsp each	ground nutmeg and cinnamon	2 tsp each
2	oranges, juiced	2
1 tsp	orange zest	1 tsp
8	fresh Scotch Bonnet or habanero chiles	8
¼ tsp	coarsely ground black pepper	¼ tsp
¼ cup	freshly squeezed lime juice	60 ml
to taste	salt	to taste
⅓ cup	dark Jamaican rum	85 ml

1. Preheat oven to 350°F (175°C). With a sharp knife score pork on fat or skin side, making diagonal cuts about ¼ inch (.6 cm) deep at 1-inch (2.5-cm) intervals. Place pork, scored side up, in a roasting pan and add stock. Cover and bake until done (1–1½ hours), then remove from oven and allow to cool slightly. Remove pan juices and set aside.

2. In a blender purée remaining ingredients except rum. Spoon purée over roast. Return to oven, uncovered, and bake for another 50 minutes, basting occasionally with liquid in pan. When done to taste arrange pork on a platter and keep warm.

3. Degrease reserved pan juices. In a medium saucepan over high heat, reduce juices to about ⅔ cup (150 ml). Skim fat from roasting pan and add any juices remaining in pan to reduced stock. Add rum and cook over high heat, stirring constantly, for about 3 minutes. Strain and pour over pork. Serve hot.

Serves 6 to 8.

BAYOU BARBARY JAMBALAYA

This rice and seafood dish is a Cajun classic suited to bayou-country tastes.

¼ cup	oil	60 ml
1	onion, chopped	1
6	green onions, including tops, chopped	6
3	celery stalks, chopped	3
1	bell pepper, seeded and chopped	1
8 cloves	garlic, minced	8 cloves
1 tsp	crushed dried hot chiles	1 tsp
¼ tsp	coarsely ground black pepper	¼ tsp
½ tsp	sugar	½ tsp
¼ tsp	dried dill	¼ tsp
1 cup	long-grain rice	250 ml
4 cups	chicken stock	900 ml
3 cups	cooked crabmeat	700 ml
2 lb	cooked shrimp	900 g
2 lb	fresh clams	900 g
½ cup	minced fresh parsley	125 ml
1 tsp	minced cilantro (coriander leaves)	1 tsp
to taste	salt and coarsely ground black pepper	to taste
to taste	cayenne pepper	to taste

1. Heat the oil in a heavy pan and add the vegetables, garlic, chiles, pepper, sugar, and dill. Sauté for about 3 minutes, or until the vegetables are soft. Add the rice and stir to coat evenly with the oil.

2. Pour in the chicken stock. Bring to a boil; reduce heat, cover, and simmer for an additional 30 minutes, or until the rice is almost tender.

3. Stir in the crabmeat, shrimp, clams, parsley, and cilantro. Add salt, pepper, and cayenne to taste. Cover and continue to simmer just until the clams have opened and the rice is tender. Serve at once.

Serves 8.

Georgia Rabbit and Oyster Gumbo

This peppery meal-in-a-pot has its roots in West African cuisine. Traditionally it is served over boiled rice.

1	rabbit, cut up in 6–8 pieces	1
2 qt	chicken stock, heated to boiling	1.8 l
¼ cup	oil	60 ml
½ cup	unbleached flour	125 ml
½ lb	okra, trimmed and sliced	225 g
1	green bell pepper, chopped	1
1	onion, chopped	1
1 stalk	celery, chopped	1 stalk
½ tsp	cayenne pepper	½ tsp
¼ tsp	thyme	¼ tsp
¼ tsp	salt	¼ tsp
¼ tsp	freshly ground black pepper, or to taste	¼ tsp
1 pt	bottled oysters, drained	500 ml
as needed	hot-pepper sauce	as needed

1. Put rabbit and stock in a large pot and simmer for an hour, skimming occasionally. Remove rabbit with a slotted spoon and let cool. Keep stock warm. When rabbit pieces are cool enough to handle, bone rabbit and reserve meat. Set aside.

2. Heat oil in a large skillet. Stir in flour a bit at a time, whisking to break up any lumps. Cook until mixture turns brown (about 10 minutes), stirring constantly.

3. Add okra, green pepper, onion, and celery to flour mixture in skillet. Lower heat and cook until vegetables are tender (about 10 minutes), stirring frequently.

4. Add contents of skillet to stockpot. Add cayenne, thyme, salt, pepper, and rabbit meat; bring to a boil, lower heat, and simmer 5 minutes, skimming occasionally. Add oysters, remove from heat, cover, and let stand 10 minutes.

5. Serve in large soup bowls, adding hot-pepper sauce to taste.

Serves 4 to 5.

RED BEANS AND RICE LOUISIANE

Serve hot-pepper sauce with this New Orleans classic.

1 lb	dry red beans	450 g
2	meaty ham hocks	2
8 cups	beef or chicken stock	1.8 l
4	bay leaves	4
½ tsp	thyme	½ tsp
1 tsp	cayenne pepper	1 tsp
2 tsp	freshly ground black pepper	2 tsp
1½ lb	andouille or other hot sausage	680 g
2 cups	chopped onion	500 ml
½ cup	chopped celery	125 ml
1	bell pepper, chopped	1
1 bunch	green onions, chopped	1 bunch
1 tbl	minced garlic	1 tbl
to taste	salt and pepper	to taste
to taste	red wine vinegar	to taste
4 cups	cooked hot rice	900 ml

1. Wash beans and soak overnight in water to cover. The next day drain beans and rinse. Place beans, ham hocks, and stock in a heavy stockpot. Bring to a boil and skim any scum that collects on the surface. Reduce heat to a simmer and add bay leaves, thyme, cayenne, and black pepper. Simmer for 30 minutes.

2. Chop sausage into ¼-inch (.6-cm) pieces. In a large skillet on high heat fry sausage for 5 minutes to brown. Add chopped onion, celery, bell pepper, green onions, and garlic. Cook for 15 minutes, then add to the simmering pot of red beans. Continue to cook beans until they are soft (about 1 hour more). Allow beans to cool; refrigerate, covered, overnight or for up to 4 days.

3. When ready to serve, bring beans to a simmer. Season with salt, pepper and vinegar to taste. Place about ½ cup (125 ml) on each plate and spoon beans over rice.

Serves 8.

BLACK BEAN CHILI

The black beans in this chili show the influence of South American cuisine.

¼ cup	dry sherry	60 ml
1 tbl	olive oil	1 tbl
2 cups	chopped onion	500 ml
½ cup	chopped celery	125 ml
½ cup	chopped carrot	125 ml
½ cup	red bell pepper, seeded and chopped	125 ml
4 cups	cooked black beans	900 ml
2 cups	chicken stock	500 ml
2 tbl	minced garlic	2 tbl
1 cup	chopped fresh or canned tomatoes	250 ml
2 tsp	ground cumin	2 tsp
4 tsp	chili powder	4 tsp
½ tsp	dried oregano	½ tsp
¼ cup	chopped cilantro (coriander leaves)	60 ml
2 tbl	honey	2 tbl
2 tbl	tomato paste	2 tbl
as needed	grated onion, for garnish	as needed
as needed	chopped fresh hot chiles, for garnish	as needed
as needed	grated Monterey jack cheese, for garnish	as needed
as needed	yogurt, for garnish	as needed

1. In a large, heavy pot, heat sherry and oil over medium heat and sauté onions until soft but not browned.

2. Add celery, carrot, and bell pepper and sauté 5 minutes, stirring frequently.

3. Add remaining ingredients, except garnishes, and bring to a boil. Lower heat and simmer for 45 minutes–1 hour, covered. Serve garnished with grated onion, chiles, cheese, and a dollop of yogurt.

Serves 6 to 8.

CHILI CERVEZA

Beer and freshly ground cumin give distinction to this all-beef chili.

as needed	oil	as needed
6 lb	beef chuck, cut into ½-inch (1.25-cm) cubes	2.8 kg
4 cups	minced onion	900 ml
⅓ cup	minced garlic	85 ml
3 cups	beef stock	700 ml
3 cups	flat beer	700 ml
1½ cups	water	350 ml
¼ cup	chili powder	60 ml
6 cans (15 oz each)	tomatoes, crushed	6 cans (430 g each)
⅓ cup	tomato paste	85 ml
1½ tbl	minced fresh oregano	1½ tbl
3 tbl	cumin seed	3 tbl
to taste	salt	to taste
to taste	cayenne pepper	to taste
as needed	cornmeal	as needed

1. In a large, heavy skillet over moderately high heat, warm 3 tablespoons of the oil. Brown beef in batches, adding more oil as necessary and transferring meat with a slotted spoon to a large stockpot when well browned.

2. Reduce heat under skillet to low. Add onion and garlic and sauté until soft (about 10 minutes). Place in stockpot along with stock, beer, water, chili powder, tomatoes, tomato paste, and oregano.

3. In a small skillet over low heat, toast cumin seed until fragrant. Grind in a blender or with a mortar and pestle. Add to stockpot. Bring mixture to a simmer. Add salt, cayenne, and more chili powder to taste. Simmer, partially covered, until beef is tender (about 1½ hours). Add more stock if mixture seems dry. If chili is too thin, stir in up to 2 tablespoons cornmeal and cook 5 minutes to thicken. Serve hot.

Serves 12.

CORN MUFFINS PICANTE

Corn muffins with character—that's what you get when you add fresh jalapeño chiles to the batter.

1 cup	yellow cornmeal	250 ml
1 cup	unbleached flour	250 ml
1 tbl	sugar	1 tbl
1 tbl	baking powder	1 tbl
½ tsp	salt	½ tsp
1–3 tbl	minced fresh jalapeño chiles	1–3 tbl
¼ cup	minced onion	60 ml
1	egg	1
⅓ cup	oil	85 ml
1 cup	milk	250 ml

Chile-Lime Butter

½ cup	butter, at room temperature	125 ml
1 tsp	freshly squeezed lime juice	1 tsp
¼ tsp	lime zest	¼ tsp
¼–½ tsp	cayenne pepper	¼–½ tsp
¼–½ tsp	ground cumin	¼–½ tsp

1. Preheat oven to 375°F (190°C). In a medium bowl combine cornmeal, flour, sugar, baking powder, and salt. Stir in the jalapeño chiles and onion. Make a well in center of dry ingredients.

2. In a medium bowl beat egg; slowly beat in oil and then milk. Pour mixture into well and stir just to combine. Do not overbeat. Pour batter into well-greased muffin tins. Bake until slightly brown (12–15 minutes). Remove from tins while still warm.

3. Meanwhile, to prepare Chile-Lime Butter, beat butter until light and fluffy. Beat in remaining ingredients. Spoon butter into a crock and serve with warm muffins.

Makes 12 muffins.

Rolled Salsa Bread

This easy recipe is good hot or cold, by itself or as an accompaniment to a meal. If you're feeling energetic, substitute homemade bread dough for the frozen loaves.

1 pkg	frozen bread dough (2 loaves)	1 pkg
2 cups	Salsa Frita (see page 24)	500 ml
4 tbl	minced cilantro (coriander leaves)	4 tbl
8 cloves	garlic, minced	8 cloves
1	egg white, lightly beaten	1

1. Thaw dough and roll out each piece into a rectangle about ½ inch (1.25 cm) thick.

2. Spread half of salsa over surface of one piece of dough, leaving a 1-inch (2.5-cm) border all around. Sprinkle half of cilantro and garlic over salsa. Starting with long edge, roll dough jelly-roll fashion. Pinch length of seam to seal. Place seam side down, and coil roll around itself like the shell of a snail. Repeat with remaining piece of dough. Set rolled loaves on an oiled baking sheet.

3. Brush surface of each rolled loaf with egg white to create a glossy finish. Leave loaves in a warm place until doubled in bulk (from 1–4 hours, depending on temperature and humidity of room). Bake at 350°F (175°C) until loaves are well browned and sound hollow when tapped lightly (45 minutes–1 hour).

Makes 2 loaves.

Variations **Rolled Salsa Bread with Cheese and Onions**

After spreading dough with salsa, sprinkle ½ cup (125 ml) Swiss or mozzarella cheese and ½ cup (125 ml) minced onion over surface of each piece of dough. Roll dough and bake as directed.

PREPARING ROASTED CHILES

If you have sensitive skin, wear rubber gloves while peeling chiles.

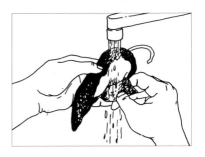

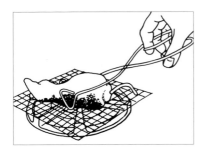

1. Blister chiles over a gas or electric burner covered with a metal screen. Turn frequently with tongs. The chiles are done when the skins are charred and blistered. Some parts of the chile will be black. Take care not to burn through to the flesh. Remove blistered chiles and place immediately in a plastic bag to steam for 10 minutes.

2. When chiles are cool, hold them under cool water and peel the skin from the chile, starting from the stem end.

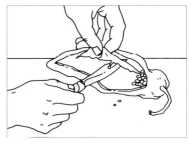

3. With a small, sharp knife, cut open the chile. Remove the veins and seeds. Wash out the last of the seeds under running water. Blot excess water from chiles.

HUEVOS HABANEROS

In this version of a Mexican classic, the eggs are poached in the salsa. If you prefer your salsa cool, fry the eggs in hot oil or butter and spoon chilled salsa around them immediately before serving. Serve eggs atop tortillas that have been lightly fried or warmed on a hot, ungreased skillet.

3 tbl	oil	3 tbl
2	onions, chopped	2
10 cloves	garlic, minced	10 cloves
1–2	fresh habanero chiles, minced	1–2
1 stalk	celery, chopped	1 stalk
1	bell pepper, seeded and chopped	1
4	tomatoes, chopped	4
½ tsp	ground cumin	½ tsp
2 tbl	minced cilantro (coriander leaves)	2 tbl
½ cup	minced fresh parsley	½ cup
1 tsp	sugar	1 tsp
2 tbl	distilled vinegar	2 tbl
to taste	salt and freshly ground black pepper	to taste
to taste	crushed dried hot chiles	to taste
8	eggs	8

1. In a large, heavy skillet over medium heat, heat oil and sauté onions and garlic until soft, 2–3 minutes. Add remaining ingredients except eggs and cook over moderate heat, stirring occasionally, until a thick sauce is formed (about 35–40 minutes).

2. When ready to serve, turn up heat to make sauce quite hot, stirring constantly to prevent scorching. Crack eggs on top of salsa, cover with a tight-fitting lid, reduce heat, and poach eggs to desired doneness. Gently spoon eggs onto a heated serving platter and spoon sauce around them.

Serves 4.

Enchiladas con Pollo

Using a good-quality canned enchilada sauce cuts the preparation time for this southwestern favorite.

1 tbl	butter	1 tbl
⅓ cup	chopped onion	85 ml
2 cups	cooked, shredded chicken	500 ml
8 oz	canned stewed tomatoes	225 g
¾ cup	salsa (see pages 22–27)	175 ml
1 can (4 oz)	diced green chiles, drained	1 can (115 g)
¼–½ tsp	chili powder	¼–½ tsp
to taste	salt and freshly ground black pepper	to taste
1 can (11 oz)	enchilada sauce	1 can (315 g)
8	flour or corn tortillas	8
⅓ cup	sour cream	85 ml
¾ cup	shredded Monterey jack or Cheddar cheese	175 ml
as needed	chopped green onions, for garnish	as needed

1. Preheat oven to 450°F (230°C). In a large frying pan, melt butter. Add onion and sauté until softened. Add chicken, tomatoes, ½ cup (125 ml) of the salsa, the chiles, chili powder, and salt and pepper to taste. Heat through. Keep warm over low heat.

2. Cover the bottom of an 8- by 12- by 2-inch (20- by 30- by 5-cm) baking pan with half the enchilada sauce.

3. One at a time, dampen each tortilla with water and heat on both sides in a hot, ungreased frying pan until soft and pliable.

4. Place ¼ cup (60 ml) of the chicken mixture on each tortilla and roll; place in baking dish. Top with remaining enchilada sauce, the remaining salsa, sour cream, and cheese.

5. Cover and bake until heated through (15 minutes). Serve garnished with green onions.

Serves 4.

COLIFLOR ROJO

Although cooked vegetables are an important part of authentic Mexican meals, unadorned vegetables are a rarity. The art of dressing up plain vegetables to create something much more special is a hallmark of Mexican cuisine. This recipe combines two distinctive flavors and colors to make a handsome presentation.

1	head cauliflower	1
1½ cups	Salsa Frita (see page 24)	350 ml
2 tbl	crumbled feta cheese	2 tbl

1. Break cauliflower into flowerets. Heat salsa and keep warm.

2. Steam cauliflower until tender (about 9–12 minutes); do not overcook.

3. Arrange the cauliflower in a serving dish and top with the warm salsa.

4. Garnish with the crumbled feta cheese and serve.

Serves 4 to 6.

SALMON SEVICHE

Colorful and zesty, this south-of-the-border specialty features fresh fish "pickled" in a marinade of lime juice, onions, and chiles. This recipe uses fresh salmon, but white-fleshed ocean fish or shellfish also makes delicious seviche (see photo on opposite page).

1 lb	salmon, cut into small cubes	450 g
10	limes, juiced	10
½	white onion, thinly sliced and separated into rings	½
1	tomato, peeled and diced	1
2	canned jalapeño chiles, seeded and chopped	2
2 tbl	oil	2 tbl
2 tbl	vinegar	2 tbl
2 tbl	chopped cilantro (coriander leaves)	2 tbl
as needed	lettuce leaves, for lining plates	as needed
1	avocado, sliced	1

1. Place the fish in a glass bowl. Pour enough lime juice over the fish to cover it, and marinate at least 4 hours or overnight. Stir occasionally to be sure all surfaces of the fish are "pickled."

2. Add the onion, tomato, chiles, oil, vinegar, and cilantro; mix gently. Refrigerate another 2 hours before serving.

3. Place the lettuce leaves on chilled plates and spoon seviche on top. Arrange the avocado slices over seviche.

Serves 4 to 6.

CHIHUAHUA CHILAQUILES

This Mexican stew works just as well with pork roast or cooked chicken or turkey.

2	onions, diced	2
4 cloves	garlic, sliced	4 cloves
2 tbl	oil	2 tbl
6	dried New Mexico chiles, chopped	6
2–3	jalapeño chiles, sliced	2–3
7 cups	beef stock	1.6 l
6–8 cups	cooked, shredded chuck roast	1.4 l–1.8 l
10 oz	frozen corn kernels	285 g
1 can (15 oz)	plum tomatoes, drained and diced	1 can (430 g)
1 tbl each	cumin seed and salt	1 tbl each
¼ tsp	freshly ground black pepper	¼ tsp
½ tsp	hot-pepper flakes	½ tsp
6	corn tortillas, cut into thin strips	6
1 cup	sour cream, for garnish	250 ml
¼ cup	sliced green onions, for garnish	60 ml
6 sprigs	cilantro, for garnish	6 sprigs

1. In a large saucepan over medium heat, sauté onion and garlic in oil until softened and translucent (4–5 minutes). Add chiles, stock, beef, corn, tomatoes, cumin, salt, black pepper, and hot-pepper flakes. Reduce heat to low and simmer, uncovered, for 45 minutes.

2. While chilaquiles simmer, heat oven to 350°F (175°C). Toast tortilla strips on a baking sheet in the oven until lightly browned, 12–15 minutes. Set aside.

3. Serve chilaquiles in shallow soup bowls, topped with toasted tortilla strips, sour cream, green onions, and cilantro sprigs.

Serves 6.

SWEET HEAT: DESSERTS AND NOSHES

The search for something hot doesn't have to stop just because the main course is over. As you'll see when you sample the recipes in this section, sweetness and lightning offer a satisfying solution when you're hankering for dessert or a between-meal nosh.

Chilied Fruit Refresco

Lime, ground chile, and salt complement the sweetness of fresh fruit to make an unusual hors d'oeuvre as well as a healthy snack or simple dessert. This combination is the typical mixture served by street vendors in Mexico, but you can use whatever is in season.

as needed   watermelon   as needed

cantaloupe

honeydew melon

mango

papaya

fresh pineapple

jicama

fresh coconut

limes, for garnish

salt, for garnish

ground mild or hot red chile, for garnish

1. Remove seeds and rind from watermelon, cantaloupe, honeydew melon, mango, and papaya; peel pineapple and jicama; crack coconut and peel away brown inner skin. Cut all fruit into bite-sized pieces and arrange on a platter with cocktail picks or on individual plates.

2. Squeeze the fresh limes over the fruit and sprinkle small amounts of salt and ground chile over the fruit to taste.

The number of servings will depend upon the variety and quantity of fruits used.

Jalapeño Thumbprints

The chile filling in these cookies provides a refreshing change from sugary confections.

½ cup	butter, softened	125 ml
¼ cup	firmly packed light brown sugar	60 ml
1	egg, separated	1
½ tsp	vanilla extract	½ tsp
1 cup	sifted unbleached flour	250 ml
¼ tsp	salt	¼ tsp
¾ cup	chopped pecans	175 ml
as needed	Jalapeño Jam (see page 93)	as needed

1. Preheat oven to 350°F (175°C). In a medium bowl thoroughly cream together butter, sugar, egg yolk, and vanilla. Sift flour and salt together and add to creamed mixture.

2. Form dough into 1-inch (2.5-cm) balls. In a small bowl beat egg white. Dip each ball into beaten egg white, then roll in chopped nuts. Place 1 inch (2.5 cm) apart on ungreased baking sheets. Press thumb gently into center of each ball.

3. Bake until light golden brown (10–12 minutes); cool slightly on racks. While cookies are still warm, fill centers with Jalapeño Jam.

Makes 24 cookies.

JALAPEÑO JAM

Serve these punchy preserves with cream cheese and crackers for an appetizer, with bagels for brunch, or as a condiment.

1 each	red and green bell pepper	1 each
5	fresh red or green jalapeño chiles	5
6 cups	sugar	1.4 l
1½ cups	distilled white vinegar	350 ml
6 oz	liquid pectin	170 g

1. Purée bell peppers and jalapeño chiles in a blender or food processor (see below). In a 6-quart (5.4-l) saucepan combine puréed peppers and chiles, sugar, and vinegar; bring to a hard rolling boil and boil 1 minute. Remove from heat and add pectin; mix well. Skim foam from surface with metal spoon.

2. Pour into hot, sterilized jars. Wipe rims of jars with a clean cloth. Seal jars with canning lid and screw top and process in a hot water bath for 5 minutes or allow jars to cool and then store in the refrigerator.

Makes 6 to 7 half-pints (250 ml each).

PREPARING CHILE PURÉES

Use caution when puréeing fresh or dried hot chiles.

1. Remove stems and seeds (see page 28) from chiles. If desired, briefly soak dried chiles in a small amount of warm water to soften them.

2. Place chiles (and soaking water, if used) in a food processor or blender and chop to a smooth purée.

3. Remove lid from blender or work bowl and remove puréed chiles, keeping your face well away from any fumes arising from the purée. If the fumes are persistent, turn on the kitchen exhaust fan.

4. Thoroughly wash hands, work surfaces, and utensils.

Bombay Delights

Meant for an adult's seasoned palate, these crispy cookies are spiced with curry powder—a mixture of cumin, coriander, tumeric, fenugreek, ginger, chiles, fennel, garlic, cinnamon, salt, mustard, cloves, and black pepper. Serve the cookies with fresh fruit, tea, or dry white wine.

1 cup	unsalted butter, at room temperature	250 ml
2 cups	firmly packed dark brown sugar	500 ml
2 tsp	vanilla extract	2 tsp
2	eggs, beaten	2
1½ cups	unsalted peanuts, chopped	350 ml
¼ cup	golden raisins, chopped	60 ml
3 cups	unbleached flour	700 ml
½ tsp	baking soda	½ tsp
1 tsp	baking powder	1 tsp
½ tsp	salt	½ tsp
1 tbl	curry powder	1 tbl

1. In a large bowl cream butter with brown sugar. Add vanilla and eggs, then mix in peanuts and raisins.

2. In a medium bowl sift together flour, baking soda, baking powder, salt, and curry powder. Add flour mixture to butter mixture and combine well.

3. Form dough into 2 cylinders, each about 1½ inches (3.75 cm) in diameter. Wrap individually in waxed paper and freeze until firm.

4. Preheat oven to 350°F (175°C). While cookie dough is still frozen, cut each cylinder into ¼-inch-thick (.6-cm) slices. Bake on ungreased baking sheets until lightly browned (12–15 minutes). Let cool on sheets about 5 minutes, then remove to racks.

Makes about 48 cookies.

Index